Titles by *Langaa*

T0198529

Oriki'badan

Emmanuel Fru Doh

Langaa Research & Publishing CIG
Mankon, Bamenda

PUBLISHER:
Langaa RPCIG
(*Langaa* Research & Publishing Common Initiative Group)
P.O. Box 902 Mankon
Bamenda
North West Province
Cameroon
Langaagrp@gmail.com
www.langaapublisher.com

Distributed outside N. America by African Books Collective
orders@africanbookscollective.com
www.africanbookscollective.com

Distributed in N. America by Michigan State University
Press
msupress@msu.edu
www.msupress.msu.edu

ISBN: 9956-558-88-5

Dedication

To all my teachers, foremost, especially
You Headmasters Bilong and Tachang of R.C.M. Buea town—
60s,
And the likes of Mrs. Ekema, Mrs. Tigem, and Mrs. Anoma.
Then you that Marist paradigm—Norbert Simms alias *Crobo,*
Of Sacred Heart College Mankon, Bamenda, of a gone-by era,
And the likes of Mr. Ralph Awa, Pa Mbuye, and Mr. S. T.
Njong,
And then, in particular, those who trained me at the University
of Ibadan, Nigeria.
In an African world tormented by political minions and na-
tional traitors,
Looters of the peoples' coffers, their hopes, and opportunities
to live,
I met at Ibadan distinguished yet dedicated professors.
Professors, fearless, who encouraged you to soar regardless of
themselves—Osundare
Professors who challenged and were not afraid to praise their
students—Izevbaye
Professors, true examples, who were proud of their students
and their efforts—Okpewho
Professors who worked hard, devoted to their students' work
and progress—Ashaoulu
Professors, true mentors, role models, parents even—
Ogunyemi
Academic giants who were yet humble and willing to serve—
Ayo Banjo.
Numerous they were, alas those names I cannot all include here,
But my gratitude to you all as I sing your *oriki,*
Distinguished high priests and priestesses of academe
That from you others may learn and benefit, especially
Those vessels resounding with "bigmanism" and nothingness
In other corners of Africa thrashed by political myopia and
kleptocracy.
May your story of devotion and service to humankind defy
time.

Preface

Many people come into the world, stir up things and depart as heroes, yet far too many come in and leave unsung, in spite of their wonderful services to humankind. In the former case, we have examples of politicians and entertainers, and in the latter group examples of the religious, health workers, and teachers. Alas, how consoling it is that the Master rewards, abundantly, those who merit it, whether the world notices them or not. This is the spirit that bore the poem "Oriki'badan."

My Nigerian sojourn, but especially my on and off experience at the University of Ibadan in the 1980s, left deep impressions on my psyche, and, to a significant degree, remodeled the manner of man I have become. I had waded through a country—Cameroon under Ahidjo—that in spite of all, bathed me in the rivers of patriotic waters, and a foreign university that instilled in me determination and hard work as the twin paths to personal and universal success. When Ibadan finally regurgitated me, I was a new man with a new sense of the world, a burning will to serve, and a re-enforced sense of God, the latter quality having been planted and watered earlier on in life, while a child growing up, by my late father—Pa Philip Doh Awah.

And so away from the University of Ibadan (U.I.), out of the city of Ibadan herself, and away from Nigeria, onward I forged. But with time, it dawned on me repeatedly that at every step, virtually, my indebtedness to Nigeria, and U.I. in particular, jiggled before me as I left footprints in the sands of time. And so, every so often, my mind flashes back to Nigeria and the turbulent political climate at the time, but more so to U.I. of those years, the great and devoted professors, like sculptors, bent on polishing and transforming the budding intellectuals in their charge into brilliant authorities and resounding minds in different callings, the turbulent circumstances, socio-politically and otherwise, notwithstanding. I think of the great friends I made whom I can no longer see or hear from—because I know not where they are—yet whose names and our experiences together I continue to see, read, and feel in the pages and breadth of time stored away in my memory and in the resurging activities of younger generations. With every passing year, the tugging at my heart continued growing stronger causing me to wonder how to calm such powerful pangs of nostalgia and the debt of gratitude I have come to realize, more convincingly, that I owe. I decided then on re-living those days, even if in their faintest form while also singing about those rarely, if ever, acknowledged heroes who made U.I. the great university it was then, and I pray still is today, knowing Africa and her current leadership, unfortunately. And so how do I say "thank you" to Nigeria, how do I say "thank you" to the city of Ibadan and its citadel of learning, the University of Ibadan, other than by imitating Africa herself, the land of the talking drum, the land of griots, the land of songs and rhythm.

This volume contains my song for my unsung heroes: Nigerian authorities that allowed foreign students to benefit from great masters, and a university system distinguished by some of the greatest brains, minds, and spirits that ever walked the earth— eminent faculty and staff alike. The socio-political odds notwithstanding, these were giants that were humble; they fired every soul, directly and indirectly, upon meeting, to strive for the heights, transforming nascent minds—from Calabar to Lagos, from Zaria to Ibadan—into fierce spirits determined to learn and serve. But nobody sings of teachers: their job is "boring", generally speaking, their pay cheque, comparatively speaking, trite. Yet in their hands rests the fate of the world, the future of humankind, given the minds entrusted in their care for them to mould, which towards heaven they could direct, or else into the abyss plunge. I sing of these heroes through the eyes of yesterday, as they came across to us their initiates. My joy is that they are still the same, those that I have run into since those days at U.I., and that has been a great source of happiness to me.

I cannot call every name that made my U.I. experience, as I could be present only at certain places at certain times, not even all of those with whom I crossed paths, yet our collective reverberations as students, even when rebellious like in '82, and those of professors and staff—academic and non-academic labour alike—made U.I. to flourish, giving it its unique socio-intellectual flavor and aura. I therefore confine my effort to the microcosmic space of the Faculty of Arts, especially the English Department. Rest assured that if I had the facts, or could gather them, this would be an *oriki* of many volumes that all may be praised, so accept this humble gesture as my "thank you," to a country and its citizens, to a university system, but especially to the University of Ibadan, that gripped my heart and still holds sway to my sentiments. The University of Ibadan, like all else that belongs to today's Africa, and to humankind as a whole, may stagger some day and even come to fall short of its own image, may her children—all those who have benefitted directly or indirectly from this noble institution—but above Nigeria as a nation, never let this and her other great institutions of learning die. That will be a blow the world might never recover from.

May I seize this opportunity to thank Professor Adéléké Adéẹkọ of the Department of English at Ohio State University, Columbus, Ohio, U.S. A. for helping out with the Yoruba diacritics. I decided, however, to use these only on some Yoruba words that have hardly been spelt out in English before, or else would obviously be misread by a non-native speaker. Those Yoruba words that have too often found their way into English write-ups without Yoruba diacritics were left to stay that way in this venture.

Emmanuel Fru Doh
Minnesota, August 6, 2008.

Oriki'badan

After years and years,
Up onto the hills with fright
And down into the valleys with sighs,
Then the plateau with relief
My life spiraled, yet now
I must acknowledge that a good
Foundation will hold a lofty building;
A carefully built house will for long
Maintain its value, the storms notwithstanding.
Of man's encounter with the travails of life
In the path to transition and of the dedication
Of others to be of assistance I sing in general.
In particular, I sing of my treacherous
Encounter with a gorgon humongous in size,
That amongst brave peers in the struggle,
I had to overcome, the doors to success
Open and my welfare guarantee.
Of my quest for knowledge in particular,
Of my journey into intellectual manhood,
Across hills, valleys, rivers, and wastelands
Across vast distances in time and effort
And my encounter with some of Africa's best
Acada[1] priests and priestesses, authorities
In our unique rite of passage, I now tell.
I sing of giants, masters and mistresses at
What they did, gem-studded crowns yet
So devoted one considered oneself blessed
Their apprentice to be. So help me Shiliwa,
Fire my cerebral lobes into motion
And feed them with facts of years

The totality of which I recall no more,
Or else barely do in some cases,
With ideas fresh, potent, and moving;
For where now you reside little sister,
The future is last night's dinner and the past
Today's breakfast. Inject power then
And rhythm into *Oriki'badan*,
That Uites may be praised deservedly,
The shrine itself, The University of Ibadan,
The fiercest *acadagorn* of all,
The most daunting since Timbuktu,
The priests, chief priests and high priests extolled,
For people earth-colored say:
Tell him when his chest rises and falls,
Or else lament when the rhythm ceases,
Give praises when due before it is late
And in regret wallow. Ah-ah "UHAI"
Speed-appellation by bus conductor:
U.I.! UHAI! UHAI! UHAI! UHAI!
University of Ibadan.

But first things first: no nursery school for me;
My father had time. From work he returned
By 3:30pm and following a deserved nap
Homework time—my dreaded hour—when
He would supplement what Mrs. Anoma, Mrs. Tigem
And Mrs. Ekema had started during the day
In the Roman Catholic school of Buea Town
In the mid and late sixties. Football I preferred
To calculations, to multiplication-tables
And division—long and short.
But I was condemned: first male and for
Long the only, so best to be as pathfinder

2

And so I worked and worked; I had to work,
And hard too. I did play, and well too,
Study I was expected to do and well too,
But only a rare child loves book over play,
And I am not rare, but my best I gave
Sometimes earning rewards: a trip to the cinema,
At other times strokes of the cane, my performance
Judge and jury. It burned in the will to succeed,
The odds notwithstanding, day, night,
Season after season I toiled at my books.
Through elementary in six years into secondary;
My choice by friendship fashioned: not
Bishop Rogan's College a Catholic priest to become
And my father's prayers answered, but St. Joseph's
By the Buea Mountain, high above the sea,
Amidst lush vegetation and the sea of tea,
With that monastic air away from civilization
My great childhood friend and master storyteller to join,
Mola Benson Nganda. But Sasse was school not home
And so there were no sessions of movies narrated:
Django! Hercules! Samson! Mark Forest!
It was mainly book. This nursery with sprouting shoots,
This camp with established senior initiates,
Some dreaded and others admired differently;
The most feared, Pa Tashi, the Master of Discipline
With his cane buried in the ridge on his back under his shirt
With which to align those who derailed, and his Official
Warnings, three in number, from which to deduct twice only
And an initiate was on his way home escorted
To the Gbea[2] motor park, denied the rare chance to
Be prepared for greater things in life——expelled!
Alas, health was not to be mine, the reasons surreal:
My maiden encounter with the beyond, Africa!

3

If not the master, get his dog and the impact better yet.
My fate sealed, Pa Nyanga's prophetic decree from his
Bonduma-Molyko groove! Away from Gbea,
Else he perishes and here remains as you and the
Rest soon on transfer return to your Abakwa roots.
What tragic note, with my love for Sasse,[3]
What tragic note with my admiration for Saker[4]
What tragic note with my budding interest in
Miss Binder's palavers.[5] The policeman will
Not hear otherwise; to a new location whisked
Off, my roots, but only that, an alien by growth
Rituals and location transformed. And so Sacred Heart,[6]
A task at dawn, my health the morning dew: cold, damp,
And foggy. I staggered on, at times ignored,
And by the same at times ridiculed. But from
Those ashes, slowly this Phoenix re-emerged,
Active and excelling in all natural to the young
And exuberant; to the dismay of wagging
Tongues that savor gossip and enjoy the cross
On others' shoulders; in place my work fell after all.
Thanks to so many teachers, secular and religious,
But foremost, yes foremost, to the bald-headed
Marist Brother, Champagnat's model—Norbert Simms[7]
For trusting in me, for pushing with his might
And dragging even, when need arose, from the
Stupor by years of malady and medications imposed.
How could he, when idiots laughed and condemned,
Understand without children of his own?
Yet he felt, believed, and knew a lot more by this
Slowly rejuvenating carcass could be achieved,
And so those rare words of encouragement that
Inspired and transformed despair into a
Fortress of hope and confidence on me he showered

Fertilizing thus the shrunken roots of my psyche
That fed then withering branches and leaves of my ego
Reestablishing the once-upon-a-time Iroko.
What was his care and concern
Which he so generously heaped
On all that came his way, student or *campagnard*?[8]
Yes, goodness soars, and before kindness
And the fear of the Lord all else is trite.
Champagnat had set the rule: of service to mankind
Was to be his lonely and alienated life
And so he served, urging and guiding all and sundry.
In response, with professions and vocations I flirted:
A lawyer to become, a political scientist,
A physician, but the Master rules, and so I dreamt
Of Law even en route to camp in Nigeria,
The hour for my circumcision—the rite of passage.

Year in year out we watched them receive and train
To distinction, age-group after age-group of young men
And women, Africa's future. We waited and waded
Life's rivers all to be pronounced ready for camp
For years of training, in preparation for our
Circumcision—graduation day. Alas the hour:
The gong of the town-crier was heard, from
Village to village all over Africa, summoning us,
Our age-group, that had bode its time patiently
To begin riding west with the setting sun,
Others rode east with the rising sun
To converge at the grove for initiates,
To converge at the grove for apprentices
Africa's sacred grove—Ibadan.
With pride in our eyes we, in various villages
And clans, folded our belongings while staring

Wisdom in the eyes—father, mother, siblings.
"Your turn son to make our dreams come true.
Now go, be humble, brave, dedicated and
You shall return a man to your own *ntang*.[9]
Listen to your elders when they instruct you,
Watch their lips as they words of wisdom
In you sow. Like a calf watching its mother browse, be;
Know your guides, their likes and dislikes,
Like the back of your own very hand,
And work hard to stand out; do nothing,
No! Nothing without their permission,
Their ages and sizes notwithstanding.
And do nothing, nothing of which I your father
Mu Njoya from whose loins you sailed forth,
Or your mother in whose womb you took residence,
From whose breasts you were nourished,
From whose eyes you saw that unique maternal love
That fashioned you thus, will not approve.
I am your father because I brought you forth
From these loins, and I am proud of you, for you
Have my every word with relish, like your
Mother's *fufu* swallowed.
I knew better, but no more, not with the
Hour changing as I witness. So now you go on
And learn from masters current in the latest art, and
Tomorrow return, and our own guide be
Even as we mark time waiting for our final summons.
Are you hearing me?" "I hear you father."
"Bring my drinking horn." And from his hand
Fru mu Doh drank—the first time, confirming my
Growth and impending adulthood.
"Stretch forth your legs and be blessed."
Along with palmwined toes the words of prayer flowed:

6

"Njoya, your child is travelling, go with him;
It was you who said he would grow, grow, and grow.
He is growing just as you predicted, so go with him.
Open his doors for him; let his face shine by day like
The sun at dawn, and at dusk like the welcoming
Face of the moon that all who set eyes on him may
Wonder, may admire. Keep him safe in all that
He does until you bring him back to us
In the name of our forefathers! Amen!
Now Go!"

After days and nights of riding in dust,
And the rains suddenly lashing out as if
My determination to put to test,
Stopping only to eat and join new groups of travelers,
At last early one dawn at the threshold, a huge gate,
I stood, exhausted but excited to have arrived.
Even from a distance the camp was huge;
For security and integrity like a palace
Within a palace the camp was fenced in,
The whole three miles square.
From the gate, huge boulevards led in,
A whole mile, before spreading out in different
Directions, fibrous roots branching from tap,
Into all the corners of the camp—The University of
Ibadan.
From the twin gates—Exit/Entrance
Vehicles of all sorts, buses too, the new trend,
Transporting anxious initiates
To and fro for ten kobo only,
With people milling around in large numbers:
Spiritual leaders, initiates for the rite—men, women,
Boys and girls—the old and the new.

On, the days passed with us waiting,
Waiting for the day of acceptance—matriculation.
Meanwhile about the camp we trotted,
Idle initiates, taking in the beauty and resources,
The vastness of this initiation camp.
See the halls of residence for initiates, huge,
With rooms for thousands: Queens, Mellanby,
Tedder, Sultan Bello, Tafawa Balewa, Azikiwe (Zik)
Independence, Queen Idia, the Students' Village (Awolowo).
So shelter there was for many, and for more squatting!
See the courtyard of the administrative High Priest
With its towering clock of many faces the hour to tell
To all wherever in camp they may be, until the
Jealous trees raised high their limbs and leaves
In every direction all over the place, clouding
The sky and shielding the tower with their boughs.

Into faculties the camp was divided following the needs
Of the palaces of Africa, the needs of initiates to specialize.
Faculties subdivided into departments: my territory the
Faculty of Arts, made up of English a.k.a. *Òyìnbó*
Grammar, Language Arts, Theatre Arts, History,
Linguistics, Philosophy, Classics and more.
Nearby was the zoo, where from time to time
The king roared its satisfaction, alerting illusory
Rivals in captivity of its royal presence; the serpents
Stretching, uncoiling and creeping in glass cases,
The gorilla staring in stately defiance as orangutans
In large numbers scream and gambol about the place
Longing their way with guests to have.
With hyenas yapping about, the leopard, with night
Vision, stares on its back defiantly, a full stomach,
Even as the crocs splash their powerful tails in and

8

Out of water, the elephant trumpeting through its
Trunk at the laughing crowds of anxious visitors;
Zoology they called this specialization.
What with this city called a school? The fire brigade
Forever on the alert with their red fire vehicles
What with this city called a camp for rites of passage?
A camp with its own security department,
A camp with its own maintenance unit.
A camp with its own diviners—university hospital!
But of all, most remarkable was the student body
With its own student government: a veritable
Ministry lodged in the Student Union Building (S.U.B.).
The S.U.B., beyond furnished offices, adorned
With sumptuous restaurants and shops
From which to buy knickknacks and little gifts
For loved ones and visiting friends and family;
The many kiosks with *pepper soup* and
Home-made dishes, the *suya* men with healthy
White onion strands and tomato slices for flavor;
The many kiosks with beer and minerals
To quench the tropical thirst or else while time
In love dialogues, speculation, and idle chat
As the day wears, with swimmers in dainty
Outfits splashing in and out of the huge pool.
One could hear the slamming of the ball against
The wall in the squash room as games went on,
And hear the whizzing of tennis balls across
The courts as challenges drive over the nets,
And the crowds from the soccer field cheering on
Even as the solitary figure of an advanced initiate
Strides on towards the library his work to do,
Besides which the Taekwondo team *ki-haps*.[10]
Ah-ah UHAI! The buildings and facilities

9

Humbled initiates, making us hunger for initiation
Rites to be done with and so truly
Worthy of these facilities to feel.

Beyond the faculty structures stood the Cross
Marking the Chapel of Our Lady Seat of Wisdom,
The non-denomination chapel as well,
Then came the star and crescent moon
For *Allâhu akbar*,[11] and then the wall
For the cross not to be seen during prayers.
At last matriculation leading us into the
Chamber of Initiation. With matriculation came
Refreshing discoveries: in our ranks were
Those to be trained town criers,
Those to be trained herbalists,
Those to be trained healers
There were warriors, griots, jesters, farmers,
And hunters; all trades for the royal palaces.
And so we parted ways; initiates now belonged to
Different departments within the camp
With different programs and schedules,
With different priests, chief priests and high priests
For mentors, with priestesses and chief priestesses.
For some initiates it was the last they would
See of each other, hear of each other, talk of each other.
The days came and went like
The pages of a huge book on time and events
Being read and flipped over by the supreme deity.
And so my focus shifted and zeroed in on
The affairs of my department—*Òyìnbó* Grammar.[12]
High Priest Ayo Banjo was head.
As the days rolled by and
The gradual process of our initiation was

To begin, three acolytes in the department's
Secretariat, with time, distinguished themselves:
They listened to us initiates, doing
What they could to help us prepare.
First that lady typist whose name I never knew
Because she left before session was in full force
To give me the chance to know her better.
But I remember her words of wisdom as on
She urged me in my quest to be admitted:
"We are only flies out here" she said, "knock on
That door, step in and talk to the man you see."
My first encounter with *Bàbá*[13] Banjo, my first
Lesson in his humility as up he stood to talk to this
Young man he had never before set eyes on,
Nor did his simplicity and approachability change
When he found me, despite my lion-skin robe
And princely appearance, a stray initiate in search of a camp.
Directives he issued that brought before him my credentials
And before long had me installed, one more new initiate.
Acolytes number two and three as I met them:
There was Mr. Imona, and there was Mr. Akin Akinmutimi,
Kind souls of the secretariat of *Òyìnbó* Grammar.
To our numerous questions they listened
And gave answer as best they could or else
Sound advice. At times even with the typing
Of numerous papers they came to our rescue,
At the very least a smile, and a word of encouragement.
Though belatedly, "thank you" you two, especially,
With whom, unbeknown to me at the time,
I was to spend years, almost a decade, in *Òyìnbó* Grammar;
But you knew we were always grateful
Hence those smiling exchanges, welcomes, and goodbyes
And even the nicknames as the sessions came and went.

Beyond these, were two advanced initiates, novices,
So good they were in their endeavors
They were chosen to play priests to newer initiates
Like us. There was Remi Oriaku, quiet, gentle,
And hardworking. He helped our age-group
Until the very end of our first stage towards
Initiation—the Bachelor's Long Essay.
Then the simple and easy-going Harry Garuba,
In disposition humble, calm, gentle, friendly,
Yet profoundly knowledgeable; Garuba, never too big
For any company and so he learned
While he guided. This advanced initiate
Showed us how to speak and pronounce well,
Before introducing us to the ways of neighboring
Village—the Caribbean. He was welcoming,
Trusting, and at ease with initiates, especially
Those in whom he saw promise.
Though physically a palm tree, down below
He would stoop in the winds of friendship
And the echoes of resounding humility
With all to interact. Harry Garuba, ẹ ṣẹ![14]
Then that Phonology lady—
Another advanced initiate, rarely seen
Out of class, and so her name
Is lost in my crammed cranium tortured by time
And with countless events and occurrences laden.
But I remember her, as intelligent as she was beautiful.
She tore down the barriers to effective articulation,
Talking about "phonemes", "fricatives", and other
Words to initiates as strange as an eclipse.
She transformed *Òyìnbó* Grammar into Biology,
Making a cross-section of the human head
Down to the chest, articulators to show

And how they function to illustrate,
Thus dividing initiates' attention
Between her beauty and her intelligence.
She left camp long before Oriaku,
Long before Garuba
To we knew not where.
To these advanced initiates at the time, I say *ẹ ṣe gan*![15]
With responsibilities well performed, gently
Breaking initiates into the ways and camp expectations
Thank you so very much. Yours were roles we admired
And strove to emulate.

Yes, High Priest Ayo Banjo was head of *Òyìnbó*
 Grammar, but shortly before the session could
Take off, he was called off, a higher office to serve:
To oversee the entire initiation camp—Vice Chancellor.
This was a giant amongst giants, intimidating
In appearance, yet humble and simple before all who
Came his way—the rich and the poor, the young and
The old, the ordinary and those in offices of power.
Bàbá Banjo saw in all human beings and nothing more
And went out to serve without delay, without attitude.
One would have thought being High Priest
In charge of the entire camp one would not be able
To meet with, let alone talk to him, as is the case with
Others, hollow politicians in government especially,
One would have thought his numerous achievements
 Like hot air a balloon would have caused his head
To swell beyond measure, but no
Bàbá Banjo was concerned about what brought one to him,
And did all in his powers to be of help.
But for higher office he had to leave *Òyìnbó* Grammar
Even though his space remained—a mere formality,

He was never to return with my age-group still in camp.
We could only hear of his feats
Which came across even as Vice Chancellor.
They said, beyond administration, in book work
He was so good he even compiled a dictionary
After ordinary books no longer challenged him.
Ha-ha-ha! *Na wa-oh!* I salute you *Bàbá* Banjo.

In his place came
Bàbá Dan Izevbaye, High Priest of *Òyìnbó* Grammar,
Theory and Criticism. *Bàbá* Izevbaye,
Calm as the sea at dusk, like a very deep lake,
In his stride slow, gentle, and steady.
An ant would not die should Izevbaye
On it stride. It was as if he could see the thorns
Of life before him and so gently stepped;
A mien that belied the fiery nature of his pen,
The penetrating zooming-ins of his interpretations
That into an authority transformed him.
Yet forever he flashed that smile at all and sundry:
The smile of an authority figure that knows,
The smile of an authority figure who recognizes,
The smile of an authority figure who understands
Because he had been there and could still recall,
Because he had been there and could still
Put himself in his charge's struggling predicament.
And so that faint smile of understanding
Always about his lips hovering, the distinguishing
Factor of this academic warrior, administrative authority.
Then a piercing look as if to see one's soul, one's needs,
Then a subtle encouragement to his initiates, all of whom
He loved, for all of whom he felt personally responsible.
Izevbaye, Head of Department, Izevbaye, Dean of Arts;

A leader who had time for all. Izevbaye will listen
Intently to complaints, calmly to indignant protestations even,
Give the impression yours is most serious
And his sympathy on your side already.
Then the faculty handbook will out for him to
Crosscheck the facts and confirm your plight,
But slowly and surely a meticulously prepared document,
The handbook proves you misguided. You failed the rules
Of the game to follow, working yourself
Into a fit uncalled for: to be done in a calendar year,
With all that work, is your choice. The high priests
Of the camp knew the work load to be too intense
Hence the two-year requirement for an M.A.
Slowly and gently *Bàbá* Izevbaye proves your
Protestations baseless, leaving you embarrassed and deflated
Even as he smiles at your convinced but groundless effort.
Bàbá Izevbaye, true administrator, simplicity personified.
Izevbaye, a veritable scholar, a true professor;
A devoted mentor who would show the way then
Challenge to encourage. I salute you Bàbá!

One after the other we met the priests,
Having been prepared by advanced initiates.
Bàbá Omo Asein, like life unpredictable:
Now a smile of recognition,
Like the beauty of the sun as it climbs
To the centre of the sky;
Next a perplexing distant look
Like the rain clouds gathering.
Again the distracted smile, the message clear:
He knew how to keep initiates alert. But
Humble initiates we were,
Come rain, come sun. And so

We swallowed all, hungering for his knowledge.
He ripped apart the African novel
And fed us its innards, urging us to grow
Into masters and mistresses capable of
Dissecting content, style, and beyond. His was
A brief encounter, but he left his mark:
These writers have messages bubbling in them:
To set right the blighted portrait of our culture
As rich as the gem stones from the belly of the continent,
By alien arrogance, fired by illusions of superiority,
Into a failure transformed,
Something of which to be ashamed.
Alas we are a people with ways unparalleled
Which we must protect at all cost against invading
Debauchery in the name of civilization
And so initiates into academic warriors transformed
To do battle and save Africa and her values
Unique and intricate like the souls of our jungles
The rhythms of the changing seasons and our animals'
Callings, that our tomorrow as a people may be
Guaranteed or else degenerate into whitewashed isms
Fighting for leftovers from another's tables
Though his kitchens we furnish with nature's
Abundance—mimicking the ways of vultures
When soaring eagles indeed our ancestors were.
 Bàbá Asein, ẹ Ṣe Sar

There was *Bàbá* Amayo who was also present
As chief priest in *Òyìnbó* Grammar. Even though
I never had to deal with him, I could tell he was
No different. Forever with books in his hand
Bàbá Amayo went about camp, and at other moments
He could be seen chatting and laughing

Freely in his sacred grove even as one went by.
But quiet was his dominant mien even as he said "hello!"
To initiates like me, some of whom he had come
To know from frequently running into along
The corridors as we rushed from room to room
From lecture to lecture. Amayo, tall, easy going and
Always willing to help, his initiates said of him.
Grammar too was his concern: dissecting sentences and
Bringing out their meanings, the surface and
Underlying, since often people's pronouncements are
Doubled-faced. There is what they want you to hear
And there is what they hope you deduce since
They will not directly say it for fear of confrontation or
Going across some other line in place installed by culture,
Age for instance, or rank. He did his job well, else his
Initiates would not have said all the good they said
About *Bàbá* Amayo. *ẹ Ṣe Sar*!

Enter *Baba* Olu Ashaolu: gentle and easily
Smiling but tough. This Chief Priest was business
All the way. He showed recognition but would
Not be too familiar, his integrity to maintain.
African Theatre was his meal, his palmwine.
He ate Soyinka before sunrise, took Pepper Clark
With the sun overhead and wiped his lips with Osofisan.
He snacked on Athol Fugard before going to sleep.
I remember him for pouring praises on Soyinka
As High Priest who has done it all: playwright,
Novelist, poet, actor, teacher, musician.
I remember him for exposing Ulli Beier for what
He is, his pioneering contributions as an *òyìnbó*
To modern Nigerian theatre and poetry notwithstanding.
Ulli Beier is Obotunde Ijimere,

17

The non-existing Nigerian playwright who
Wrote *The Imprisonment of Obatala*.
No Yoruba person will call his child "Obotunde",
The reincarnation of the monkey—Beier's summation
Of the black person; no Yoruba person would
Think of the almighty deity, *Ọbàtálá*, being
Imprisoned… by whom? Ah-a! *òyìnbó*….
Even with our hospitality, welcoming him into
Our midst and doing all for him to feel at home,
Something his people do not have,
Feeding him with *àmàlà* and palm wine,
Something his people rarely do;
We let him into some of our secrets
Encouraged him our tongue to understand,
Into an authority transforming this stranger,
For him to turn around and insult us. A
Response to generosity unparalleled. He learnt
Our ways but would not our appreciation acquire;
Old habits die hard they say. Now I know all I
Need to know, now I have all I want from and about you
And so the insults begin. *Chei, òyìnbó them na wa!*
But *Bàbá* Ashaolu will not this nonsense take,
To us he made it clear: Ulli Beier is Obotunde
Bàbá Ashaolu, *ẹ Ṣe Sar.*

Enter glass-eyed *Bàbá* Niyi Osundare,
The man with four eyes, two given by *Ọbàtálá*
And two by man; high priest who looks into
The spirit world and then descends to see and deal
With human beings—prophet in the wilderness.
He breathes in oxygen but exhales poetic constructs
Garbed in Yoruba rhythms. *Bàbá* Osundare
High Priest of Stylistics, a true giant in every way,

With that distant philosophic look in his face;
Forever writing a poem in the air before
Transcribing onto his sacred page. *Bàbá* Osundare,
Looking always in the distance as if in constant
Telepathic exchange with an unseen muse,
Juggling thoughts as he walks, occasionally
Conscious of the hubbub surrounding him.
He had seen it all and was determined
Above it all to rise, and so his glance
And awareness soar in the distance,
His attention arrested by an unseen scene,
To this High Priest alone visible. His voice
Like the wind in the wilderness:
"You will hold your assegai this way,
And thrust it thus for maximum effect.
Beware of words, they are potent when well
Chosen and applied, and will go where your
Legs cannot follow." Rebel mind, his soul a
Fountain of poetic visions and ideological conflicts.
He churned out volume after volume of songs,
Some from the market place and others by the moon.
Master poet, *Bàbá* Osundare, simple, friendly,
Inspiring, devoted yet demanding.
For a lot more I remember you
Fountain of confidence and hope to all
Who came your way. His was the gift
To pull out the best in any willing initiate,
And these he loved working with
Not letting his colossal status
Come in between. *Bàbá* was a hard worker.
He left his home to his office, to class, the library,
And back home. Fearless poet who called
A spade a spade and despised the threats

Of his oppressors, severally putting even his life
On the line for his convictions.
Bàbá Osundare, town crier extraordinaire.
With that enchanted life of a seer, which forever
Seems to attract travail after travail, even to
Katrinaic levels, in the path of this poetic luminary;
For *Bàbá* Osundare to rise and overcome all with time.
Charmed life yours seems to be High Priest of poetry,
Supplied you are with the means to soar always
And emerge unscathed. Is your juju in your *dànsíkí?*[16]
In that rising front hairline that keeps the running brain
Forever cool? Else Dagda's grandson you are,
Poetry to turn into soup for *àmàlà* by mother Brigit
Prepared. It is that mien Osundare, that humility,
That simplicity, that willingness to be there for all;
Their gratitude potent prayers to the supreme deity
Who then from the stones guides your steps,
From the dust washes your feet, so with hands washed
With your fathers you may ultimately dine.

Ẹ Ṣe Bàbá!

Slowly crouching, like a tiger stalking,
His eyes slowly sweeping from left to right,
From right to left, daringly taking in his initiates.
Enter Chief Priest Joseph Egberike in charge of
Òyìnbó Drama. To meeting sessions *Bàbá* Egberike
Walked in with calculated steps, a performer already
Possessed, eyes hidden behind dark glasses
The trance-like gaze not to betray to the uninitiated;
His stalking approach, like an aiming hunter about to
Let go a shot, like a lion about to dash for the kill,
Held initiates spellbound in anticipation.

In an awe-laden moment of expectation, after a brief
Rite of salutation, he would begin, in a trance,
Vomiting Shakespeare like a regurgitated meal
In that season of scarcity before starving initiates,
And one could see the passion, his love for
What he did in his every strain. He quoted from
History to tragedy, from comedy to tragicomedy
To make his point. *Bàbá* Egberike lapped Shakespeare
Like a lion at noon, after a meal, water from
An African river: effortlessly and with relish.
And because of his mastery, the ease with which he
Commanded forth lines, he left initiates mesmerized
After each meeting. One volume was never
Enough to support his point, and so we learned
The need to lean on different authorities foreign and
Domestic for buttressing our own views—substantiation!
We learned to sieve the material and extract that of value:
Beware of a wife's fear else like Caesar be
Damned for ignoring Calpurnia's warnings. Study
Well your friends and weed out Iagos else
Like the Moor hurt yourself so bad some day
By murdering innocence. Know when your
Emotions to shut down and to the call of business
Answer, else humiliate yourself someday like Antony
For discarding duty for a woman's embrace,
Learn from Hamlet and do not a victim of
Procrastination be when evidence screams for
One to swing into decisive action; it is said
"A stitch in time saves nine."
Into dramatic lines *Bàbá* Egberike would soar,
Venting emotions accordingly,
Sweating as he wrestled with ideas
Like a performer in a trance, and then gently

He would begin his descent into reality
With his body relaxing: the point home,
The kill between his jaws,
The handkerchief across his brows.
Once more out of class the master of lines
Would glide in victory daring us with the
Slow pendulum-like movement of his head,
His stare of victory, aware his point
Has been made. It was now our turn to
Learn by emulating the master. Egberike,
Juggler of dramatic lines, mill that churns
Forth Shakespearean meaning; Master of
Òyìnbó Drama proper. *E̩ S̩e Bàbá*!

Enter *Bàbá* Isidore Okpewho, High Priest and gateway
Into Orature, custodian and advocate general of Africa's
Epics, Master of oral messages, of diverse concerns
And presentation patterns, of the tortoise
And the hare, of griots and the kora, of epic
Characters and fantastic deeds. The perpetrator
Of tales, with Sundiata, like other names from
The Mandingo resonating. *Bàbá* Okpewho
This bridge between times; Okpewho, he that strings
Generations into a united whole and philosophical
Force; *Bàbá* Okpewho alias *Bàbá* Class.
This High Priest radiated confidence, and
Traditional sophistication in all that he said
And did. He took life with a certain ease
As if to the pantheon itself he belonged,
O̩bàtálá's son especially forged to keep his name
And those of minor deities and distinguished heroes
Resonating. Okpewho present and about all

Yet at a distance as if not to soil something
About him that he held sacred. Even then
Simple, soft-spoken, perceptive, patient and
Understanding of his initiates' plight, *Bàbá* was
Above anything corny; you had to get close to him
To better know him, the distance a safety gauge
From so much around he considered beneath him
Not out of arrogance but the need to be decent,
Not out of arrogance but the need to respect himself.
With that deportment, he taught by example
Even before exposing like the veritable authority
He is, the facts of the oral traditions of Africa,
Earning the respect and admiration of his initiates
And peers. Beyond his confident and noble deportment,
Initiates loved his brown horse which shimmered
In the sun; this noble warrior had accomplished so
Much so soon. A true high priest who defended
The lore of his people in the face of alien
Propagandist: yes, the epic exists in Africa.
His name crackled in the domain of Orature
Like a flash of lightning in the consciousness of all,
And his works rumbled like thunder
In the belly of dark pregnant tropical skies
Just before a downpour.
Orature, a dance whose steps he has mastered:
Head of Department and Commander in Chief of Oriki,
Of Ijala, repository of the griots and teller of tales.
Bàbá Okpewho has given order to Orature,
For all to see and recognize Africa's cultural wealth.
In Orature like a dominant lion Okpewho has mapped
His territory; on the hills of the Savannah he stands
Daringly, yes he can hear the crocodiles splashing
In the river, the hippopotamuses chasing about

And the gazelles trotting, other roars in the distance;
Yes, in the distance. He shakes his mane and
Strides off. Okpewho, standard bearer of Africa's
True portrait: the land of tales and performances,
The land of instruments, songs, and dance.
Okpewho kind at heart and always willing to
Help better another person—friend or stranger.
Okpewho, colossus that to help mankind is always
Creeping instead of towering his full height, yet
Never will he accept he is doing anything extraordinary.
Bàbá Class, ẹ Ṣe Sar!

There was Mama Chikwenye O. Ogunyemi, chief priestess;
Into camp she brought in foreign culture—Harlem
Renaissance. In the face she slapped us with Toni Morrison,
Whose works seemed to bring Mama Ogunyemi to life;
There was Imamu Amiri Baraka, Alice Walker. It was she,
Ogunyemi, to make initiates look at women differently;
It was she Ogunyemi who wanted to be accepted for the woman
She was and nothing more—Womanism!
It was she Ogunyemi who loved the essence of epistolary
Novels, novellas, and like *Bàbá* Achebe, to her initiates,
Exposed Joseph Conrad's true nature
Even as he insulted my people and called nature
The heart of darkness, with Kurtz degenerating
Into worse than the "natives" themselves…
And those grey strands that crowned her effort.
She refreshed our minds with the female
And black predicament in the world,
But she always came back home to Africa—Bessie Head.
Easygoing, gentle smiles, and a good listener, but *oya*
Watch it; she, principled and tough like a metal bar.

When Mama Ogunyemi says 9:00am, it is 9:00am,
Not 9:01am; fellow initiate Jude Agho will bear
Me witness here. But the initiates understood
Her toughness and the training she was giving us.
Only those willing to work dared near Mama.
She made us understand there was no room
For nonchalance in the world if we were to succeed.
It was only a front, and we knew it. This was
A mother who would not spare the rod and
Spoil her initiates. Deep down indeed, she was
A true African mother: her initiates, her children,
Gave her life meaning. This chief priestess bold and daring
Was a devoted worker, attention to details her trademark.
Her horse was a strange one, yellow in color—unique—
As if to forewarn of this extraordinary priestess.
Rarely did she smile with her initiates, it was gentle
And brief, but we knew she cared and would work hard
If you would. Working with Mama Ogunyemi
Meant success guaranteed because of her devotion;
It meant bringing out the best in an initiate
And it meant thorough supervision.
Mamma C. O. Ogunyemi, *ẹ Ṣe Ma*!

Mamma Molara Ogundipe-Leslie, chief priestess
Of words and songs—Modern African Poetry.
Enchantress from the belly of Mother Africa,
With poetic rhythm in her stride
With rhyme in her lion-skin clothes,
Princess of the songs of modern Africa
With a contemplative look on her face,
Forever searching for meaning from the
Lines of poetic spontaneity laced
By strands from the daily events of

The undulating landscape of Africa's
Socio-political panorama.
She did not talk much,
But the brain in her head like the talking drum
Was heard booming during sessions.
Our encounters were rare and far apart,
But whenever to the department she came,
She would start from the north to the south,
East to the west, riding in defiance the poetic
Winds of all who challenged Africa, exposing
The contents of poetic strains, leaving us gaping
At another woman to whom poetry was palm wine,
Another woman, an authority in her own right.
This chief priestess was business all the way.
She would recognition show, but a smile
Out of the question, or else faint and brief.
Ogundipe, *e̩ S̩e Ma*!

At the time High Priest and Head of the department,
Bàbá Dan Izevbaye encouraged initiates that
Would benefit from other relevant stuff
Not taught in his department go to
Other departments for select courses.
And so from *Òyìnbó* Grammar I found myself amongst
Initiates in History contacting Chief Priest Mojuetan
And others. But *Bàbá* Mojuetan left a mark on my
Mind; his name and his ways I remember well:
With his *dàn̩s̩íkí,* and his left hand in his pocket,
 Pulling up his trousers, his books
Under his left armpit, his chalk in his right hand,
Bàbá Mojuetan walked casually to sessions,
Taking in the buildings and students
As if newly painted, like wraiths in his path,

With a gentle nod of recognition here and there.
To him nothing was important than giving a successful
Lesson. He lectured and left us with references,
Further readings to do on our own. He taught and
Taught, loading initiates with facts and work to be done.
It was like he had to tell the story before it was late;
He spoke about Africa's past and left us proud:
The ancient empires and Kingdoms of Oyo, Ghana,
And Ashanti, of what Africa was before her invasion
By outsiders. He looked and sounded like he was
Joking but then the storm of knowledge poured
And poured, clearing the dark sky that loomed
Over his balding forehead, the class, and Africa's portrait,
Leaving initiates gasping for breath. Forever
Looking simple, deceptively so, the trademark
Of Ibadan chief and high priests. The tie to them meant
Nothing other than an occasional
Confirmation of our contamination. Or else
Always simple in appearance but sophisticated
In train of thought. Great minds that know
Are not like empty containers; their substance
Keeps them forever humble, forever simple,
For ever willing to serve; *Bàbá* Mojuetan, *ẹ Ṣe Sar*!

High Priest Bodunrin, another encounter in a foreign
Department "tormented" us with Philosophy—"Appearance
And Reality," and so on—forcing us to begin thinking
And grappling with abstractions. A tough encounter it was,
But determination led us through. *Bàbá* Bodunrin,
Another true authority, and like them all soft spoken
And always willing to help. My sojourn in the
Philosophy Department was brief compared
To my stay in a department like History,

And so the names of others have faded away.
Even so, you who taught us Ethics,
Fair-skinned, gentle, quiet, and focused.
And then you the *òyìnbó* chief priest who taught
Me the Philosophy of Language,
To you all of Philosophy I say *ẹ Ṣe*.

In Classics we ran into High Priest Kujore,
Lean, tall, and authoritatively daring in looks,
Who spiced his moments with Greek and Hebrew.
This Chief Priest in a class of his own: simple,
Traditional, knowledgeable, demanding, father-like.
Forever lost in the clouds of intellectual abstractions
Behind the blinds separating the hour from the classical,
In lofty conversation with classical personages.
A 50% in Kujore and you had to be
Good indeed, and so he strengthened our
Understanding of so much in the classical domain:
Horace, Homer, Longinus, Aristotle, and the list continues.
How diversified initiates became who followed High Priest
Izevbaye's advice to attend sessions in other departments.
And so we left Classics shaken to the core by the grades
But versed in matters classical. I, one of only two
Above 50% of about forty-eight initiates, if not more.
It was my last romance abroad as I returned to my
Department determined to forge on, fortified with
Charms, amulets, and powerful incantations from
History, Philosophy, Classics, Politics, and the like.
Bàbá Kujore, *ẹ Ṣe* Sar.

Beyond those in whose classes we sat,
Beyond those permanently in *Òyìnbó* Grammar
To plod and trudge alongside us aiding our progress,

There were priests, chief priests, and high priests
In other departments we saw only from a distance;
There were those in other camps of whom we heard only,
Never in a classroom did we sit to listen to them.
But our priests and chief priests
Those present and those away were all the same.
Of those absent and their techniques
We learnt accordingly upon recommendation
By reading of their deeds and what they had to say,
Otherwise given us by word of mouth
By those present, their lives and travails,
In which they distinguished themselves.
Their works we also read,
Acquiring their lessons on life, about the world,
About Africa, her conflicts and woes. Literary
Legends they were, their knowledge bestriding large
Numbers of conquered cultures, their academic feats
And achievements told us like the tales of old,
Myths of origins and great wars of yore about the world,
About humankind's achievements and failures.

In this class was Chief Priest Femi Osofisan alias *Bàbá* Femo,
His specialty, beyond languages, was performance—drama.
His department was close by, and his voice
Could be heard as he trained his initiates. I was never
In his class in person, yet how his works moulded thought.
The stage was his dish from which he ate *àmàlà*,
In command of theatre corridors like a drinker
His palm-wine gourd, his buffalo horn.
The stage was his shrine, his sacred groove;
His plays, cowry shells which he tossed around
And predicted what the future held for politics,
Bad governance, and politicians. Like a farm that

Transforms a grain into corn-cobs, Osofisan's pen
Purged out play after play, compass to his society
Foremost, the wind vane to Africa at large that we
May know where we came from and see where we
Are headed and so find our way out of ideological
Sandstorms from alien deserts invading our cultural
Oasis and blinding African princes, stripping them of
Who they are and their duty to society, Africa's princesses
Stripping them of their dignity and role as noble spouses
And devoted mothers of society. *Bàbá* Osofisan so
Against injustice you would fight four robbers alone;
You must destroy yesterday's bad ways and purge your
People of the *Kolera* of corruption for tomorrow
To dawn with a smile, its teeth radiating the many colors
Of the sun king, the moon queen, the river goddess.
Bàbá Femo, brave warrior in defense of the downtrodden;
Poetry is his bow and the words his arrow
Targeting Africa's kleptocrats that before dusk
We may smile once again. Griot for honesty, praise-singer
Of the upright, milestone to the Kingdom of Uprightness
Along the landscape of Africa's political meandering;
It may take time for that hour to rise from your labour
But it will come as many hear your songs echoing
And choke on their deeds remembering your stage lines.
How being of help to your initiates seemed a primary
Goal of yours, leaving many humbled and
Grateful by your example, *ẹ Ṣe Bàbá*.

There was *Bàbá* Soyinka—Wole Soyinka. Larger
Than life were tales and lessons about him and
His deeds: he could swallow a volume whole
And vomit it again whole, his system having
Extracted everything of value. This high priest

Of many faces, who could smile and frown
At the same time, laugh and weep at once, look
Behind and in front in the same glance;
Himself a true son of the same initiation camp,
Later to go across large bodies of air and water
To challenge even foreign high priests and deities.
He returned victorious from the land
Where the people have lost the color of their
Skin, the land where it is said people speak
While refusing to open their mouths,
From the land where people speak as if their
Tongues were sore and the words pepper,
The land where it is said people speak
Through their nostrils and laugh as if in pain,
The land where many know not how to be friends,
The land where this stranger was so poorly treated,
His skin colour, flu to the society, even over a
Telephone conversation she wondered the color
Of his skin, determinant to tenant-ship.
God must be stupid then: only valleys no hills,
Summer without winter, men no women,
Dry land only, away with the waters and marshlands—
Daylight only, away with the moon and stars.
Myopia, plain stupidity in this hour. Notwithstanding,
Bàbá Soyinka proved himself twice through
Excellence in all that he did; they agreed he was
Extraordinary, this "West African sepia"!
He returned to camp from time to time
And news of his arrival would gallop about
Alerting all, in every nook, of his inspiring presence.
His feats we studied, trying to make sense of his riddles,
Trying to get meaning from his woven diction
And tormenting lines as he played *tabala*[17] with

Their tongue out of which, like mud, he built castles
For the confident to investigate and the daring
Attempt to re-decorate. With his ensuing fields
Green and woodlands towering with ideas we laboured
To see whither they would lead. From *The Man Died*
We marched on through the forest dancing,
To *Idanre* across *Seasons of Anomie* and beyond,
In our quest for meaning and wisdom.
The effort rendered hairless premature scalps
And scared us of the tassel ahead instead.
Some suggested his works for advanced initiates
Be reserved and fledglings spared the *wàhálà*,[18]
Yet on we forged, mastering his technique with time,
With words from some world beyond, with a baffling
Diction challenging to native and foreigner alike,
And then deconstructing his lines and stories until the pith we
Could undress and stare at the core of his philosophy.
His weapons top of the scale: his spears masterly crafted,
Their points sharp, and some poisoned even. These
He reserved for enemies of the land, enemies of the
Masses, oppressors of the wretched of Ọ̀bàtálá's handiwork.
Samples were shown us, crafted from the best wood,
The patterns intricate and so he could stab, jab, and thrust;
His goal the determinant of his technique.
At the very least he was confirmed a grand master.
For years we were bathed in his ideology
And scrubbed clean, made whole by his combination
Of myth and the African worldview, the world as a whole
And the manner in which he presented it. And so we ate,
Drank, and even choked on Soyinka, that exercise in
Intellectual maturity. Even in distinction his travails
Continue as he is accorded all kinds of names, from hero
Through traitor, to teacher. His pen speaks for him

Turning the Nile into blood, summoning toads into
The palace, all to free his people from bondage.
His struggle continues, forcing him in and out
Of the village from time to time: now in peace
Then at war only to return in peace again,
The rhythm of his life as onward, like many others
He forges with the search for the formula of peace
And stability amongst his people. *Bàbá, ẹ Ṣe Sar.*

Then there was *Bàbá* Abiola Irele, of whom
So much was said by other priest in *Òyìnbó* Grammar
So much so that one dreamt of meeting this warrior.
Of him tales were told: he had made the camp proud.
His was to examine others and to ensure the techniques of
Craftsmanship were followed and standards not
compromised:
That the gold smiths had not forgotten the use of the bellows,
That smelting was done at the right temperature
The god of fire consulted and placated accordingly,
The god of iron consulted and given his due respect
And forging perfected until the task took the right shape
Leaving not even children in doubt of the goal:
A spirit of birth or a spirit of death;
That the facial marks from Oyo were revealing
And so the marks from Ondo.
His it was to ensure the smiths
And members of the different guilds
Were in line with tradition, that standards may
Not fall, betrayed by personal whims.
Irele, traditionalist extraordinaire: hold the spear this way,
Put the piercing blade at this angle for such an effect,
Your design of the shaft fails to communicate personality;
What is that line for? Three steps in front and one behind?

Where is your equilibrium in technique? Dance two steps
To the right and two to the left and charge forward for
balance.
And then burry the point thus for total effect.
He too was to cross that big body of water,
Master their tongue, the secrets of their rites
Which he pitted against the time tested
Versions of the empire of old. *Bàbá* Irele,
Initiate master from yonder. His recommendations
Carried to the initiates on the wings of the wind,
The sounds of the talking drums at dusk, and
The scintillating rhythms of the kegite in the
Cold hours of the night, the threshold of dawn,
By the gong of the town-crier at the stirring of the sun.
Bàbá Irele, literary whip extraordinaire, *ẹ Ṣe Sar!*

Then there was *Bàbá* Achebe; from afar he tickled us
And we laughed and laughed even as tears of realization
Glided down our cheeks. Through his words we
Learned to speak with meaning; we learned to speak with
Authority, this master of words whose strength was
And remains how simple yet how profoundly loaded
His diction has been. To him the message is pounded *yam fufu*
And proverbs the soup, the fish, the goat leg and pepper
That furnishes the way for delicate speech
To be well received by the listener.
Like the son of the new god whose
Messengers flung our villages apart,
He spoke in parables, in lines rich in proverbs that
Established his authority. His foremost cry announced the
Impending death of the kingdom in the coming
Of strangers who pretended friends to be,
Only to disrespect the laws of the land and make

All apart to fall. They caused sons to challenge their
Fathers, wives their husband's authority to defy;
Age to them meant nothing: to elders they spoke
Without respect. Through them, disrespect and lawlessness
Established themselves in power. When children
Their parents and elders disrespected, they claimed
It was the ways of the powerful stranger. But only a fool
The wicked ways of another would emulate;
Only a simpleton the ways of his people abandons
For another; only a moron the words of his parents
Disposes of for someone else's.
Bàbá Achebe spoke and spoke from stride to stride
To sow confidence in us, confidence in our ways,
And caused the initiates and other priests to think,
To weigh all on scales, of our values, to see the nonsense
We have become, degenerating with every passing day.
His seed of pride in our ways was planted and watered
With time and lush proverbial examples.
High priest in his own class: simple but profound.
Distinguished offspring from Africa's gonads
Left to tell the tale as it should be: Africa has values
Tested by time, which were only disrupted as a result.
The struggle has been long and the effects devastating,
But the weeds must be uprooted for the harvest
In time to be rewarding. In every way then we must be
Aware of where we went wrong so as to know where
And how to turn back to the noble ways of our ancestors
Who can no longer recognize us from the land of the dead
As they look back wondering what befell their progeny.
Bàbá Achebe, *dalu*.[19]

Then there was *Bàbá* wa Thiong'o,
High Priest of the hills and the valleys,

With rivers between. Like *Bàbá* Achebe he wept
For our land torn against itself by strangers
Who pretended friends to be. With firearms
Our land they stole, in the process brutalizing us
And vandalizing out property, before camping us in
Detention units, sterile pieces for new villages.
Wa Thiong'o lamented the destruction of villages of old,
With sacred sites and shrines from our forefathers inherited,
The destructions of families, with wives seized and tortured
With husbands jailed away from loved ones, until some,
Unable to bear the strain, let infidelity in with devastating
Results: the collapse of families, the fall of houses,
The end of clans, and our ruptured culture, the white man's
Gift in return for our welcome and hospitality.
What did we do to deserve such horrors?
Wa Thiong'o wept; we begged and prayed them
Leave us alone, in vain. And so the men of the hills,
The men of the valleys—brave women too—rose
In unison under one name—Mau-Mau—to oust the monster,
To oust the stranger-turned-traitor and exploiter.
The battle was long and fierce, with the drums rumbling,
Swallowing lives, of the young, of the old, of true patriots,
The one after the other like time souls, like the *mboma*[20]
Chickens. Our heroes, tired but determined, won at last,
The land was and remains ours, our Papa's land
In which we have been since creation,
But the casualties were numerous; the after
Effects devastating. To free the future
Bàbá wa Thiong'o preached decolonization.
Like *Bàbá* Achebe, his words were down to earth simple,
But his stories of horror left one frightened to the core:
The viciousness of power over innocence, visitor
Over host—Colonization! Wa Thiong'o has struggled

The filth to wash off his body by disowning "James,"
By wading back into the Gikuyu hour or yore,
But with the scars as evidence of the encounter,
And the sounds of strange gunfire he hears at dawn,
Of women screaming and villagers wailing at dusk,
As moronic dictators cling to power planting disorder
And chaos in the human fields of hope, Kimathi's wake.
The invader, like a wasp, left within us his sting
And its pain, the consequences, continues to spread,
And spread, and spread, leaving wa Thiongo's
People piebald. Like a true leader and our brave warriors
Of old, wa Thiong'o has fought for long and hard too,
But he refuses his exhaustion to show as he marches on
Urging each new generation to remember who they are,
Where they came from, no matter where they find
Themselves in this cheating, lying, globalized world
Of today. It is like my own father always said Gikuyu
Warrior, "It is the fool that goes to the farm
And will not return home with the harvest."
For the effort *Bàbá, ni wega.*[21]

Then there was Ferdinand Oyono of Naopoleonic
Tongue twisted into Elizabethan diction
For us to understand, alas another African to us,
Like the rest, had to speak in a tongue of the *'care*[22]
Even with Kiswahili that could have been taught us
Or Lingala the language of rhythms, this pain
In the side of my identity. Oyono, it was,
Another son of the soil who showed us clearly
The game played Africa by Gaullist vandals
The game played Africa by Leopold II which
Climaxed on Bismarckian soil where it was agreed
Africa to slaughter to placate the Western gods of

Greed, scavenging, and exploitation. They proceeded
Africa to butcher without my father's voice,
Africa to disembowel without my mother's say
Let alone the future of her children consider.
Our land transformed into Sankara's casino chips
Gambled with by Western socio-economic hit men
Messengers of civilized Machiavellians preaching
Democracy while imposing despotism in Africa
Through brainwashed puppets clinging to power
Their sole goal, patriots into fleeing game they turn
Hunting them abroad—politico-economic pollination.
In suits with briefcases cooked schemes loaded
For the rescuing and civilization of "tribal" Africa,
The imbalanced terms of trade notwithstanding.
Africa's wealth was all that mattered, the strength
Of her sons, the strength and beauty of her daughters
Even as their land was arbitrarily taken from them
And divided by and between warring civilized nations
Like His robes by and between crucifying soldiers,
This persecution and crucifixion of my people
This extermination of our roots as the mighty and
Industrialized globalize the struggling and agrarian.
But let time tell; did not the slave's rod, a serpent,
Swallow almighty Pharaoh's? Yes, for the love
Of their queen free lands were acquired from
Impoverished villagers, their labour forced from
Them with Napoleonic strokes and lies about home
Overseas, for which alien frontiers more of our
Sons, even after the trade, still had to die
All for a ridiculous medal *sans valeur*
With hours in the sun waiting for the commandant.
Our high priests, beyond *The old Man and the Medal*
Echoed these facts as they pointed

To the scars on Africa's hide today: anger, despair,
Disillusionment, chaos, fragmentation, hatred, wars,
Alienation, disease, poverty, unquenchable thirst,
There at the spot itself where the fountain surges
Forth cooling alien tongues that turn around to
Babble nonsense about Africa, about Africans.
Little wonder Can Themba's will was to die,
While another illustrious son of Africa,
Meja Mwangi, begged to be killed quick.
The chaos is still on even after decades and
So the struggles to identify ourselves in the face
Of civilized aggressors, *Père* Oyono, *akeva*.[23]

There was *Bàbá* Okigbo,
Star that is gone,
Who washed his hands too soon
And so dined with the elders in the land yonder,
Even before his sun had risen to stand over head,
Even before the buds of his seeds their heads could raise
From the subsoil. This intellectual, then soldier
After his conscience, what noble service
Alas at what price, to deprive mankind of more.
In your wake your words echoed and from
Heavensgate through Mother Idoto cracked
As you reminded us of the sacredness of duty,
The meaning of conviction, the true value of service.
You stretched out your hands, pointing your pen
To where this invasion by holy water will lead
Even as our shrines were being questioned
Even as our shrines were being judged
Even as our shrines were being desecrated.
Yours was a painful lesson which on a
Pedestal left you as signpost for future generations

To judge for themselves. Okigbo, torchbearer
From the East whose pride in your people
Was so highly valued to deprive us of the wisdom
You could have fed time, untimely felled by
Some general finger, some general trigger, some
General pellet, all alien weapons and philosophies
Ambushing our values. You live on Okigbo
In your ideas than those booming sounds of political
Power that maimed us so. Oh star that is gone,
  Bàbá Okigbo, *dalu*!

There was *Bàbá* Armah, from the land
Where gold flowed like a river
Until they themselves called it The Gold Coast,
Whose anger was cascading, and with
Cataclysmic consequences as first he struggled
The fragmented pieces of his nation's id to reconstruct
Hoping to re-emerge with the Africa of the trans-Saharan trade
In gold, salt, and more by Moorish caravans and princes.
Like many others, this noble son returned to his native
Soil to serve only to be slapped in the face by
Postcolonial political minions, decadence,
Corruption galore and the overwhelming belief in cargo
Even as established institutions decayed for want of
Patriots. For trying hard to serve his people a
True son of the soil, like many others, is stigmatized and
So a nation of resources with all the manpower crashes.
This was the climax and it all started two thousand seasons
Earlier, peaking in the fragmentation of order.
Hence the sad conclusion: the beautiful ones are not yet
Born else not with this status quo scores of years after.
You have done your part and still you forge on
With the struggle. You may not reap the rewards in full

But tomorrow's Ghana, tomorrow's Africa,
Will forever remember brave men like you who
Staked everything for the children of tomorrow
When hopefully Africa, like Penelope, will regain
Her pride when her genuine princes and princesses,
Like Ulysses, will return in large numbers from alien
Shores and like Rawlings and Sankara lead rebellions
That will flush out docile dinosaurs that have been
Nothing but bootlicking morons unable to think
For the good of the sons and daughters of Africa.
Men, some even grey in years turned mere
Political houseboys to foreign leaders; men
Who think it is alright for Africa to continue
Aping after foreign standards because they fear
Too lose their presidencies which serve no other
Purpose than the welfare of these cursed figure heads,
Else like Sankara suggested, only to be murdered by you
Puppet whom he trusted and called friend,
What is this debt that for decades and apparently
For ever will continue emasculating Africa?
Why is it so hard for Africa to emerge with her own
Currency backed by her natural wealth instead of stooping
To siphoning foreign treasuries? Why are African leaders
Without vision? Why do they think governing means
Antagonizing their own people to the point of bringing
About civil wars that serve no good? Ah Africa, how
You weep for true leaders, real men and women with
visions
Conjured by their people's predicaments, instead
Of these post-colonial traitors to Mother Africa,
Liabilities to the continent who cannot see
Beyond their stomachs and infested egos.
Bàbá Armah, *medagse!*[24]

41

In this same group of High Priests not present
In person, there was *Bàbá* Okot p'Bitek whose songs
We could hear in the distance as Lawino lamented
The collapse of order with the coming of *acare*
With Ocol no longer himself, cold and with an appetite
For alienated women who, claiming sophistication,
Carried fire in their mouths going about
Puffing out smoke like nocturnal masks of secret cults;
Women have turned blood-sucking vampires with
Bloodied lips and the decay of death about us all.
But Ocol is no better, not sympathetic
The once-upon-a-time true husband now
Maddened by alien ways lashes out in response.
True though, he has no more Acoli good sense
Of time and value, his life now programmed with
Exact hours for everything he indulges in—tea, coffee—
Nor does he joke anymore. This brain-drain,
This stifling of talent and truncation of self esteem
As sons and daughters are estranged from their roots
By foreign trends that slowly nibble their way in
Like a disease, only to be noticed when full-blown,
You fought against until the end. *Bàbá* p'Bitek,
Acoli prince and vanguard in lamenting Africa's
Decadence, malaria by parasites inflicted.
Bàbá, afoyo.[25]

Then *Bàbá* Denis Brutus, the caged bird, sang songs
Of love, of pain, of fear, to Martha. He will not lose
His mind in the oppressor's coop, so this lark sang,
His sanity to maintain and tomorrow in perspective lodge,
Defeating his oppressors, those of the continent.
In vain they hoped for one more rushed burial

In vain they dreamt of one more asylum case
As his songs mental freshness maintained and fueled
Life with a reason not to die—Martha's smiling visage.
From *Bàbá* Fugard we learned of the pass laws for
"Kaffirs,"
"Kaffirs" whose land it was, whose wealth it was even with
Machine guns rat-tat-tating and felling our sibyls,
Dehydrating the land of its intelligentsia,
Of its fountain of ideas in dealing with impostors...
And the world's politicians with veto powers looked
On preaching diplomacy and the need for tact, even as
Africa's children are slaughtered and streets turned
Into rivers of blood as man hunts down man because of
Greed buried deep in the colour of their skin.
"Kaffirs", brave men and women that stood their
Ground with war songs in defiance, with the front line
Falling and falling with each spontaneous uprising
The front line falling and falling with each massacre,
Response to the will of the downtrodden,
With songs of exile from foreign shores
As the struggle for freedom as human beings
Continued in the face of the civilized.
From *Bàbá* Peter Abrahams of the richness of our
Earth we learned: our rocks shafted out by our heroes
Confined in mine-wards away from family, away from
love,
The reassuring coursings of wifely fingers
That played tunes of endearment on a husband's back.
They dug and dug, sacrificed tubercles,
Miles down into mother's womb
And the earth coughed up riches by the hour,
Day after day, yet our people remained paupers
In sweated seas of shimmering wealth.

Time passed….
And so U.I. laboured, through illustrious priests
And so U.I. laboured through eminent chief priests,
Through celebrated high priests
And initiates present, to instill in the future
The ways of our forefathers. Of these priests, those present
On campus taught; those away were invited for sessions,
Or else of their feats we heard, read, and learned.
We toiled at our tasks by day and by night, thinking
Of nothing but the feathers of success to be accorded
At the setting of our training sun. It was tough and
Oftentimes lonely, but there were peers alongside
From whom one found courage, the courage to face
Our brave and distinguished priests, the courage to
Face the prospects of our impending circumcision.
From camp one could simply leave as an initiate,
Having undergone the rite of passage and emerged
Victorious—Stage one—or return for another rain or two
And leave an accomplished superior initiate—Stage II—
Else return for about four more rains and emerge priest.

First, then we poured in just initiates to be,
Boys and girls on daily routines, drinking in wisdom
From our elders about the land, about our values,
The world of the gods, of invading alien customs
And the consequences on our people, our land, our values.
The pace was fast and we needed ways to remember
The wealth of information. Sometimes in despair we
Looked at each other, but determined onward to forge.
I remember some who close by me stood, shivering
Together in the frigid dark nights with NEPA[26] gone
Berserk; the hot dry noons with Oberdam shrinking,
Those hungry days with *eba* for meal and nothing else,

Those tiring weekends when our understanding
Was challenged: research papers in large numbers
To write and submit. There was, amongst many,
Joshua Cheng, playful, humorous, but determined;
Victor Fomunyam, master of wit and tongue in cheek;
Morenike Soyinka, calm, profound, and friendly;
Seyi Balogun, happy-spirited, friendly and confident;
Oyinda Sodipo, quiet, stern, yet friendly and outgoing;
Remi Raji, calm, contemplative, penetrating and determined;
Victoria Attat, dedicated, spirited, and hardworking;
Asi Eta, fun-loving, daring, teasing, and confident;
Kunle George, cool, quiet, and easy going;
Constance Oki, gentle, friendly, spiritual;
Felisha Akpan, mature, tranquil, and controlled.
Great souls all with whom one stood side by side
Blows from our priests to receive and deal with;
Our fun, laughter, and determination made our burden,
The task of digging through volumes for buried wealth seem
Light; the process was not fun, but the end—initiated
Men and women, graduands—kept us going.
There was senior initiate Eldred Green with his white beetle,
Built for Nigerian roads. Simple, gentle, warm and
Understanding—700 level— Eldred Green,
Our personal friend and inspiration, that warm smile.
Many more there were, alas time has partially erased
Distanced lobes of the loaded tabula rasa,
For which I regret. Even then, in my mind's eye
I see those faces every now and then, determined youths,
Their beauty tantalizing, their courage inspiring.
Together we stood, laughing, stressing, studying,
Critiquing, guiding each other through three rains,
Until our hour came and down the aisle we walked
For all to see and shook the hand of the chief-high priest.

At last, bravely from camp we strode,
Successful initiates, tassels to the left, determined life to face.
And so we bid our farewells to the great rooms of U.I.,
Her beautiful courtyards and the swift and wide corridors of
time,
Her distinguished priests, chief priests, and high priests,
The huge bellies of welcoming hostels, the beautiful
Student life on campus, the bewildering nights of darkness,
The rich flora with huge trees and drooping boughs for shelter
The rolling hills with trimmed lawns here and there,
The wet season and the cascading downpour of soothing
Showers from the heavens drumming lullabies on our roofs
And bringing sleep and rest to our challenged minds and
bodies,
Yes, even the weeks of dryness and draught,
The shocking truths of student protestations—Femi Falana.
Farewell to U.I. with the winds of fate pollinating
Us in different directions to different corners of Nigeria,
Africa, and beyond. Along with Cheng and Fomunyam
On our horses we mounted, Magi from the East,
Retracing our steps, equipped by Ibadan to deal with
The Etoudi Pharaohnic lodge of Babatouraism segued by
Deceit and connivance into Mvondoism alias *chop broke pot*
And the bootlicking sect of idiots playing *big-man*
And Women, or better still playing *Oga* (Ogre)
In to which their inhumanness transforms them in their
Buffoonery of nationhood building and governance.
But life away from camp alienated the trio;
They say man plans but the supreme deity disposes.
Our callings suddenly different, and so in unknown
Directions we headed, but our hearts the days in camp
Never abandoned. Alas only brief spells of reunion
Were we to experience. Hence the years passed,
Transforming us into spouses, parents, and more,

Widening the distance and estranging further.
But that is the stage of one's life, onto it actors enter
And stay, others enter stay for a while and then exeunt
Yet others refuse to enter at all. No matter, the play
Must on; the Director is in total control.
Reconciled to this reality my solitary destiny then
I chose to face, but not without the pangs of nostalgia
For our days together as an indomitable team
With fresh travails brought on by the tides of time
The cycle—professional and otherwise—fulfilling,
Yet with every challenge, vocational especially,
With every dispute before Babatoura, before Mvondo,
The more I saw, experienced in nuances, how well the
University of Ibadan fashioned me. I wondered
What more secrets she held for me, if only I had
Dared into stage II, the Chamber of Inquisition,
Into which only willing and determined initiates
Are introduced following their circumcision.
The desire to discover burned in me;
I must return and uncover more from Ibadan's belly.
But then, I remembered, my search for Fomunyam
Had been in vain, the story was different;
Same for Cheng, a different and interesting
Route he had chosen—like father like son.
How was I to do battle without my wingmen?
How was I Ibadan to face without a complete team?
But my heart was ablaze. I dropped all—love and
Family—and left, sacrifice beyond measure,
Back to camp, resolved the secrets of stage III
And not just II to uncover before returning home.
And so once more from loved ones, family bliss,
Onwards I tramped—back to camp—Molete, Ibadan,
U.I.! UHAI! UHAI! UHAI! UHAI!

I knew my way about camp this time,
But that was as easy as it got; all else
Challenging, if not more than it was before,
The chief priests and priestesses, the high priests
More so. I could feel my heart pounding in anticipation
Of 700 level courses, but I calmed myself—
UHAI is my turf— what about the brand new?
The novices at this level were few, the best from
Around, to be accepted into UHAI's Chamber of Inquisition:
The Master's class. There were young men and women.
Anticipation and uncertainty burnished into their features
As we waited. The chief priests and high priests
Were for the most part the very ones
We had seen around, but their mien different.
They smiled, but one could see their smiles tasted bitter.
They talked, but their words were few and chosen for
precision.
They said what they had to say, they meant what they said;
The air was thick with attitude: we would be busy, and
No nonsense would be tolerated. We were now mature
Novices in the Chamber of Inquisition and there would
Be no room for initiation practices: pampering and
babysitting.
We read and read and wrote and wrote,
Books upon books and papers upon papers,
Lamenting the work load and the level of perfection required.
We had to be in camp for two rains, but could leave after
One if we could do all that was of us required said the
Handbook. The thought alone was scary but I knew
It could be done; it had been done.
The pace was fast, the work intense, leaving one
With no time about camp to stray. Away with parties,

Away with fun trips, away with movies on campus;
It was all work, with seven research papers in two weeks
For those frightening take-home exams.
Late in the lonely midnight hour one could hear the
Sound of silence, else the fading tune of some soft music,
Or better still, listen to the sound of a lone manual typewriter
Rattling away in the hopes of meeting some fast approaching
Deadline, and none of the occupants at camp
Took offence at this otherwise disturbing chatter.
They understood: tomorrow, if not already,
Their turn, and one could use all the support.
Old boy, take am easy-o-o[27] went the salute and praise
Of a floor mate, a nocturnal returning late from
Some entertainment with work on standby. Every man or
Woman to his or her own schedule so beware the apparent
Air of nonchalance within the postgraduate hall,
Each had his or her private schedule and kept to it in silence.
The night turned into day repeatedly, weeks into months
And then the end of one rain. Dissertations to be typed, edited,
Submitted, and later bound; the camp was in frenzy with
Every passing hour until from one's hands the volumes
Are accepted by the department. But not before Oty Laoye,
Just above 700 level, priestess in the making, had helped me
Like a very sister. Oty, easygoing and smiling all the time,
How we grappled over a title for my dissertation until
At last inspired she threw in "the Wilderness," and struggle
For an effective title was over. Oty, willing to help even
To sparing me her expensive horse to ride, like Eldred Green
Did with his beetle before initiation, when time went faster
Than my exhausted legs could carry, when time went
Faster and deadlines could barely be kept. How much I owe
These great partners in struggle, friendships forged and
Emerging from nowhere other than the will to graduate

Together—*esprit de corps*—as priests. At last, from me
These volumes are accepted and under a dark and stormy
Sky, the downpour heavy with the thunder rumbling and
The lightning flashing in shredded streaks, signed by
Chief Priestess Mama Chikwenye Ogunyemi.
It had been long and exhausting, with necks turned giraffe-
like
And eyes owlish from the strain and work-imposed fasting,
But alas all was at an end and we waited for the grades.
It had to be a 60% or more to jump the M.Phil into the
beyond,
The Chamber of Invocation, where meditation is introduced
And the secrets to invoking forces beyond now exposed;
The chamber where spells by authorities are cast.
On forged this griot, one of only four and to this day
One can hear the joys of success in the corridors
Of the department, the rooms of the hostels, in the
Leaves of the trees, the whispering winds of the camp,
And in the ticking of time. But that was not enough;
I had to be a priest, the fleece my father requested;
The red feather that accords respect and dignity
Even on campus from other initiates and novices,
Approval even from other priests. I had to know
The secrets of the Chamber of Invocation where
Chief priests are formed and taught the secret rites
And sacred chants of invocation that into authorities,
High priests, transformed them, according them the right
To philosophize. I had put on some of the distinguishing
Yet humbling robes of graduands, B.A., M.A., and
The M.Phil for others, but that rare robe all in flames,
The bright and intimidating red robe of Ibadan priests,
Like that red feather of distinction in the Bamenda Grassfields,
The zenith for many, is held in awe by all. And so
I advanced, energized by thoughts of the sacrifice

Of loved ones, the camaraderie of fellow initiates.
This was a different and grand phase with all in order.
Things being equal, I could choose to work hard and
Graduate soon, or laze about and stay on forever.
How like the rest I worked both day and night
Fired on by thoughts of love and family seemingly
Abandoned for knowledge's embrace alone.
I pored over and wrote, and pored over and
Wrote for seminars in number numerous,
With chief priests playing nonchalant, ruse to
Instill independence and confidence, daring even.
Slowly but surely the hours ticked by
And with each so much work accomplished,
With High Priest Okpewho in total control
And advanced novice Kolawole Gboyega
Peer in travail, working by, on whom to fall
For assurance, moral support, as in each other
We confided our hopes and challenges.
Onward this duo forged, slowly learning the steps
Of the dance, the rhythms of the tam-tam,
The chants of all, the sounds of the different animals,
Their tracks and habits; the poise of the master hunter,
Whiz of Ijala, songs of Ogun, the gestures of praise-
Singers, maestros of oriki rhythms, fountains of praise.
And so time passed as the seasons came and went,
The dusty dry winds of the harmattan stretch,
The bloated rain drops of the Monsoon winds.
After all the rains——three——the hour came
And High Priest Okpewho gave his approval,
My experiences in camp and field to be typed out
In readiness for submission, even as the panel
Was put in place in preparation for the *viva voce*.
For the weeks before the final rite of passage

Into priesthood, I rehearsed the signs of the skies,
Of the weather changing, the names of weapons and
Battle strategies, the names of instruments, the different
Dances and the attendant dance steps by warriors,
I practiced the lines of songs, the names of herbs,
The role of the performer, the role of performance,
The tricks of the crouching tiger, the yapping of the hyena
The snarling of the lion-king, the fetishes of the hunter,
The steps of the praise singer, the attendant regalia,
The words of praise, the meaning of death
And the consoling rhythms of the dirge.
Thus sharpening my knowledge, my hide, in readiness
For the strokes that I must receive to be pronounced
An adult male and accomplished priest. The camp
Was alive with the buzzing of initiates and novices
Who in due course were to face the potentials of juries
When out of my tent I strode towards the department
With eyes red like a palm-wine drinker at dawn,
Like a kegite post cult session,
Like a red-scarfed pirate upon an island pause,
Like a yellow-scarfed buccaneer after a raid,
For lack of sleep as I perused both day and night,
Determined to do battle to victory or the death.
With my ink-fount boiling hot by my breast-pocket
Eyes in the distance invoking my ancestors
Escorts and companions before this awesome jury
To be, with confident strides, shield in hand,
Academic gladiator, I waded towards the tense arena
Like a lion sniffing the passing winds in defiance of alien
Male hormones violating my territorial integrity.
I was ready to do battle with a fearsome jury
With High Priest Oyin Ogunba at the head.
My last journey as a novice… time was to reveal.

And so on that fateful day, the appointed hour,
Entered *Bàbá* Oyin Ogunba to preside.
News of his achievements preceded him wherever
He went. In awe whispers reminded all of the stuff
Of which he is made. One would think him a giant
Breathing fire with eyes burning red and nostrils flaring
And venting fumes from academic wars fought and won;
One would think *Bàbá* Ogunba arrogant and haughty,
Even deadly, because of his skills and mastery of
The oral traditions. Ah! How humble are some authorities.
Bàbá Ogunba even smiled and greeted as he ambled to the
Exam chamber my budding authority to challenge. Yes,
Wisdom is humble, Wisdom is understanding, Wisdom is
Accommodating. Alas it was time, and this master of Orature,
Like a hunter crouched in his *agbádá*,[28] turned the dissertation
Over as if he had not seen it before, not true;
He had, for weeks gone by, devoured it like a bowl of *àmàlà*.[29]
He knew well every line like the taste of palm-wine.
And then he started: he drilled and drilled, question here,
Question there: answers satisfactory, with *Bàbá* Isidore
Okpewho, *Bàbá* Olatunde Ìlatunjí, *Bàbá* Sam O. Asein
As jury. By me in spirit stood sweating yet shivering
Co-novice Kolawole Gboyega (Kola wale!) who was
To be victim number two for the week. But
We strode to success before Africa's best,
From North to South, East to West,
Into irokos and baobabs transformed
By the priests, chief priests, and high priests of
Ibadan primarily, others by extension and yet
Others by association, or else they linked
Up with their works and subsequently made them guest
Lecturers or external examiners along the line.
Firsthand knowledge then we got from the best

Of the best any institution could boast of:
Of spirits that spoke like men
Of spirits that spoke like women
Of spirits that descended on us
With spears dripping ink, fresh from the
Numerous battles they've fought in academe
The numerous victories they've won
That on their faces radiated the confidence
Of mastery, and in their voices that cracked,
Like the lightning flashing in the darkest of
Stormy nights. They were mentors that chided to guide
They pushed and goaded us until we feared
The promise land at that pace not to attain:
How to wield the sword with effect,
The spear throw with poise and certainty,
Blows from the foe to dodge and how.
These were sacred authorities of the game:
The ease with which they presented their lessons,
That ease with which my mother pounded yam-fufu
That ease with which my father swallowed yam-fufu
That with which my sister *moin-moin* prepared
That ease with which my uncle swallowed *àmàlà*,
That ease with which my grandfather swallowed *eba*.
Yet we could tell how much work they had put in
And though at times we panicked,
On we forged knowing that like them we would win
And like theirs our shrines someday would be decked
With skulls of the vanquished; it was our turn to
Trudge on and learn the ins and outs of events and
Situations exploited by warriors to make men of boys
Mothers and women of distinction out of girls.

Notes

[1] At the University of Ibadan of the eighties, academics was simply referred to in short as *acada*.

[2] *Gbea* is the traditional name for Buea, a town in the South West Province of Cameroon, the former capital of that part of Cameroon that was once referred to as West Cameroon.

[3] Sasse is the neighbourhood in which St. Joseph's College is located, but it is always used to mean the school and not its location.

[4] Saker Baptist College is the name of a distinguished Baptist Secondary School for girls in the city of Limbe, Cameroon.

[5] Miss Wilma Binder, as Vice Principal of the institution, had the habit of censoring letters coming in for the girls, and those from anyone not on a list pre-approved by the girl's parents were opened. If they came from a boy and he was talking about a relationship, the girl was in trouble. Such letters were known in Saker as Palaver Letters.

[6] Sacred Heart is the standard way of referring to Sacred Heart College, a boys' secondary school in Mankon, Bamenda, Cameroon.

[7] Marcellin Champagnat was the founder of the Marist Brother order.

[8] For decades, Sacred Heart College, Mankon, a secondary school in the North West Province of Cameroon, was situated in the country, away from the hullabaloo of the budding Bamenda town at the time. During those early years, students simply referred to the surrounding neighbourhood as the "country," but they preferred the French word for it – *la campagne*. Accordingly, all those who lived in the surrounding neighbourhood were considered country folk, *les campaignards*.

[9] *Ntang* is a building in which one resides, a hut in most cases.

[10] *Ki-hap,* the yelling sounds produced by Taekwondo practitioners.

[11] *Allâhu akbar* (God is great) is a Muslim expression frequently used in a number of situations like in the exchange of greetings and even when the faithful are summoned to prayers.

[12] *Òyìnbó* is a Yoruba word used for white people.

[13] *Bàbá* is a term of respect, and endearment even, that could be equated with Grandpa for example.

[14] *Ẹ Ṣe* is "thanks" in the Yoruba language.

[15] *Ẹ Ṣe gon* can be translated in to mean "thanks a lot."

[16] A *dànṣíkí* is a Yoruba traditional garment that is wide and goes down tos the knee in length. It is worn by the male gender.

[17]*Tabala* is a children's game which requires each player to take turns tossing a clay bolus in boxes drawn on the ground. The player then skips from one box to another and in the process shifts the bolus with his or her toes while standing and hopping on one leg from box to box without the ball settling on a line, in which case the player hands over his or her turn to the next player.

[18]*Wàhálà*, a Yoruba word, here means problems or challenges.

[19]*Dalu* is "thank you" in Igbo.

[20]*Mboma* is the pidgin word for a python.

[21]*Ni wega* is "thanks" in Gikuyu.

[22]*'Care* is the contracted form of "acare" which is the term used for a white person in the Mankon language of the North West province of Cameroon.

[23]*Akeva* is Bulu for "thanks." Bulu people are found in South-Central Cameroon.

[24]*Medagse* is "thanks" in Fante.

[25]*Afoyo* is "thank you" in the Acholi language.

[26]NEPA is the acronym for National Electrical Power Authority.

[27]A pidgin expression for "take it easy."

[28]An *agbádá* is a robe-like outfit traditional to some African ethnic groups.

[29]*Àmàlà* is a dish traditional to the Yoruba. It is made from dried yam which is then ground into yam powder; it is then sieved and when needed, processed into *àmàlà*.

[30]*Ŋgui* is the word for the supreme deity, God, among the Mankon people of the Bamenda Grassfields of Cameroon.